Atwood and Eskimo
Visit a Farm

Atwood and Eskimo
Visit a Farm

ISBN: 979-8-9865768-3-1

This story was written especially
for my young friends across the road,
Amaya, Aurelia,
Cambria, and Gabriella.

Atwood and Eskimo
Visit a Farm

My name is Atwood. Our son, Neil was born in Alaska,
and some of his friends call him "Eskimo."
This story is about one autumn day at a farm.
We went there to meet the animals,
and maybe even to pet some of them.

We got to the farm just in time to watch the sun set over the pond, and then it was dark, so we played a board game, and finally went to bed.

When the sun rose the next morning, we rose with it. Eskimo and I went out to say, "hello," and started petting any animals who wanted to be petted.

Some very big birds were roaming around the farmyard.
They did not want to be petted. They spread their long
tail feathers into a huge fan, and showed–off for us.

Then, when they turned around,
I saw bright blue and green feathers shining in the sun.
These birds were Peacocks.

Free to roam, they strutted around like kings,
and each wore a crown made of crest feathers.
Some bright round spots on their tails looked like eyes.

One curious peacock strolled over to peer in at some peahens, ducks, geese, rabbits, and chickens. They had to be fenced-in, to protect them from predators.

Too bad, guys. Honk. Honk.

What is wrong with this picture?

Soon, a cat flung himself down at my feet.
He was looking for a pat, I thought.
No problem!

Now I had a handful of feathers and a lapful of cat.

Next, we met "Hammy", the pig.

He liked to be petted, and he liked to eat.
But more than anything else, he liked to sleep!

Look! . . . Goats!

They would probably like some petting, too.

I really wanted to hug a horse,
and now my chance was about to come.
We followed the animals into the barn.

This was the first time I ever had to *lean down* to hug a horse!

Eskimo shared some peppermints with the horses.

Here he is with his new BFF.

The farmers' daughters had grown up competing in horse shows – shining in horse jumping, especially.

By now, the girls had mostly moved on. But they had left the dusty old barn wreathed with their ribbons.

I think many stories have been shared in this old barn.

After tending to all the chores
that go along with owning animals,
it was a perfect place to sit and relax with friends.

Starting with thick, yummy blueberry pancakes,
and ending with a big horse-hug for me,
this day at the farm
really had done its magic!

Sad to be leaving, we took one more look at the pond, and then headed home to the city.

www.ingramcontent.com/pod-product-compliance
Lightning Source LLC
Chambersburg PA
CBHW082007140626
46553CB00020B/2670